PIANO · VOCAL · GUITAR

THE
DAVID ZIPPEL
SONGBOOK

ISBN 0-634-08057-1

Disney Characters and Artwork © Disney Enterprises, Inc

Williamson Music is a registered trademark of the Family Trust u/w Richard Rodgers,
the Family Trust u/w Dorothy F. Rodgers and the Estate of Oscar Hammerstein II.

WILLIAMSON MUSIC®
A RODGERS AND HAMMERSTEIN COMPANY
www.williamsonmusic.com

EXCLUSIVELY DISTRIBUTED BY

HAL·LEONARD®
CORPORATION
7777 W. BLUEMOUND RD. P.O. BOX 13819 MILWAUKEE, WI 53213

Visit Hal Leonard Online at
www.halleonard.com

DEDICATION

To my cherished family:

Michael Johnston
Martin Zippel
Joanne Zippel
Fred Schnitzer
Zachary Zippel Schnitzer
Erica Zippel Schnitzer

To the memory of my Mom, Doris Zippel, who would not have imagined this book but would have been thrilled by it.

And to the memory of Nancy LaMott, who would have expected it.

Thank you:

To my friend and my publisher, Maxyne Lang, whose idea this songbook was and without whose nurturing and soldiering it would not have happened in this decade. To Vince Scuderi who helped every step of the way. And to all the amazing Williamson Music/Rodgers & Hammerstein Organization family, especially Mary Rodgers, Ted Chapin, Vicky Traube, Bert Fink, Kara Darling and Cindy Boyle.

To Larry Gelbart for writing the foreword and for leading me forward with his inspiring example, brilliance, generosity and friendship. 18 years ago Larry and Cy Coleman entrusted an unknown lyricist with their precious musical *Death Is for Suckers* (which grew up to be *City of Angels*). For their astounding courage and their belief in me I will always be grateful.

To the extraordinary composers with whom I have had the privilege to collaborate:

Alan Menken, Andrew Lloyd Webber, Bryon Sommers, Cy Coleman, David Pomeranz, Doug Katsaros, Frank Wildhorn, Jim Brickman, Jimmy Roberts, Jonathan Sheffer, Lex de Azevedo, Mark Chait, Marvin Hamlisch, Matthew Wilder, Mervyn Warren, Pamala Stanley, Rob LaRocca, Todd Chapman, Wally Harper and Walter Afanasieff.

To the book writers and screenwriters who co-parent the characters who inspire most of the songs I write:

Larry Gelbart, Wendy Wasserstein, Charlotte Jones, Cheri and Bill Steinkellner, Joe Leonardo, Ron Clements, John Musker, Irene Mecchi, Don McEnery, Bob Shaw, Barry Johnson, Rita Hsaio, Chris Sanders, Phillip LaZebnik, Eugenia Bostwick-Singer, Raymond Singer, Dean DeBlois, David Reynolds, Robert D. San Souci, Brian Nissen, Richard Rich and Mark Saint Germain.

CONTENTS

BIOGRAPHY

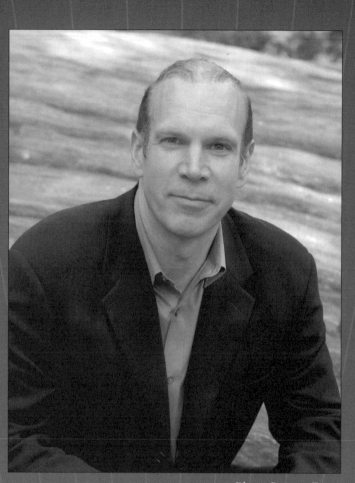

Photo: Romain Frugé

David Zippel's lyrics have won him the Tony Award, two Academy Award nominations, two Grammy nominations and three Golden Globe nominations. He is one of the few lyricists to have achieved success on Broadway, in Hollywood and in the world of pop music. His songs appear on over 25 million CDs around the world.

With composer Cy Coleman and bookwriter Larry Gelbart he made his Broadway debut with *City of Angels*, for which he received the Tony Award, New York Drama Critics Circle Award, Drama Desk Award, London's Olivier Awards and Evening Standard Award.

With eight time Oscar-winning composer Alan Menken, he wrote the songs for Disney's animated feature film *Hercules*. Michael Bolton recorded "Go the Distance" from *Hercules*, which was a #1 record and was nominated for an Academy Award and a Golden Globe. With Matthew Wilder he wrote the songs for Disney's animated feature *Mulan*, which earned him his second Academy Award nomination, his second Grammy nomination and his third Golden Globe nomination. "Reflection" from *Mulan* was recorded by Christina Aguilera and is featured on her multi-platinum debut album. Christina and David collaborated again with Todd Chapman to write the song "We're a Miracle," which was featured as the end title song for *Pokémon: The First Movie*, on its #1 soundtrack album.

His Broadway musical *The Goodbye Girl*, with music by Marvin Hamlisch and a book by Neil Simon, received a Tony nomination for Best Musical and earned him a nomination for the Outer Critics Circle Award for Best Lyrics. His lyrics for *The Swan Princess*, an animated feature with music by Lex de Azevedo, were nominated for a Golden Globe Award.

Many great singers have recorded David's songs, including Stevie Wonder, Mel Torme, Ricky Martin, 98 Degrees, Barbara Cook, Cleo Laine, Linda Eder, Sarah Brightman, David Pomeranz, Jeffrey Osborne, Boyzone and Nancy LaMott. (With David Friedman he started Midder Music, a record company created to introduce the world to the singing of Nancy LaMott.)

With Marvin Hamlisch he has written several songs for motion pictures as well as the text to Mr. Hamlisch's symphonic suite *Anatomy of Peace*. He wrote the theme song (with composer Michael Skloff) for the hit TV sitcom "Veronica's Closet." With Mervyn Warren he wrote the end title song to the Jennifer Lopez film *The Wedding Planner*. With composer Wally Harper he has written numerous songs for singer Barbara Cook, including "It's Better with a Band" from Miss Cook's live at Carnegie Hall album of the same name and the original songs for her Broadway and West End concert: *Barbara Cook: A Concert for the Theatre*. Off Broadway, Mr. Zippel has contributed lyrics to the revues *A...My Name Is Alice*, Hal Prince's *Diamonds* and, with composer Doug Katsaros, wrote the musical comedy *Just So*. A revue of his songs entitled *It's Better with a Band* played Off Broadway, at the Donmar Warehouse in London's West End, and at the Prince Music Theater in Philadelphia. He wrote the original songs for *5, 6, 7, 8...Dance!*, which starred Sandy Duncan at Radio City Music Hall.

Upcoming projects include *Princesses*, an adaptation of the classic children's novel *A Little Princess* which Mr. Zippel conceived and will also direct (music by Matthew Wilder, book by Cheri Steinkellner and Bill Steinkellner); *Buzz!!*, a musical extravaganza about the life of Busby Berkeley (music by Alan Menken, book by Larry Gelbart); *Pamela's First Musical*, based on Wendy Wasserstein's children's book (music by Cy Coleman, book by Wasserstein); *N*, the story of Emperor Napoleon and his Josephine (music by Cy Coleman, book by Larry Gelbart); and *Lysistrata: Sex and the City State* (adaptation by Larry Gelbart, music by Alan Menken). Scheduled to open in September 2004: *The Woman in White* at London's Palace Theatre. This adaptation, for which David has written the lyrics, has music by Andrew Lloyd Webber, a book by Charlotte Jones, and will be directed by Trevor Nunn. Maria Friedman and Michael Crawford are set to star.

A graduate of Harvard Law School, David is delighted not to practice law.

FOREWORD

Back in the late '80s, composer Cy Coleman and I were working on a musical comedy, *Death Is for Suckers*, a piece about the misadventures of an author of private eye novels during the filming of one of his books in Hollywood.

We were in need of two things. One, a new title (which would turn out to be *City of Angels*); the other, a lyricist to complete the creative team.

The world of the theatre being largely populated by people seeking sanctuary from security (and very often, sanity), we chose a young, untested Harvard Law School graduate, David Zippel. A barely known commodity (and for the purposes of billing, even alphabetically challenged), Zippel had made the decision upon graduation that, rather than shopping for a shingle, he would take his chances writing for the Broadway stage. A lawyer turned lyricist? It was an open-and-shut case of someone choosing rhyme over reason.

The law's loss was the theatre's gain. David proved to be an ideal collaborator. He is, first of all, fast. Not simply in the matter of the speed with which he writes; it's more about his mental quickness. David *gets it*— whatever the particular *it* happens to be. He gets the situation or the attitude his words are meant to describe. He gets the tone, the slant, the angle. He gets the character who will deliver the song and why that song has been assigned center stage. That character will be given love songs that are never generic, (although they can have their own lives, when they are interpreted beyond the wings of the theatre—or the borders of a movie screen). Most importantly, his lyrics for a character will specifically reflect whatever substance they have been endowed with by the writer of the book and the composer of the music.

The wit in David's lyrics (at once liberal and considerable), the poignancy of his poetry, become the character's, rather than David's—again consistent with the attitudes and characteristics a character has displayed in his or her spoken, rather than sung, text.

First, but not least, David is a joy to work with. He has enthusiasm. Energy bright enough to read by. He delivers. And always in a timely fashion. He takes criticism. He's just as adept at dispensing it—his own always of the constructive variety.

I suppose I could just as easily write about a flaw or two that I have detected in him over the years and several projects down the line; chinks I've discovered in the armor of this unfrocked attorney. What would he do? Sue me?

—Larry Gelbart
Beverly Hills, CA

DISCOGRAPHY
(Partial)

True to Your Heart . . . . .Raven

How in the World . . . . .Linda Eder

Plan On Forever . . . .*The Wedding Planner* Theme Song

We're a Miracle . . . . .Christina Aguilera

Reflection . . . . .Christina Aguilera

True to Your Heart . . . . .98 Degrees & Stevie Wonder

Go the Distance . . . . .Michael Bolton

No Importa La Distancia . . . . .Ricky Martin

Shooting Star . . . . .Boyzone

Reflection . . . .*Mulan* Soundtrack

There's No One Like You . . . . .Sarah Brightman

Born for You . . . . .David Pomeranz

The Story of My Life . . . . .Sandy Lam

You Can Always Count on Me . . . . .Cleo Laine

Far Longer Than Forever . . . . .Regina Bell & Jeffery Osborne

You're Nothing Without Me . . . . .Mel Torme & Cleo Laine

With Every Breath I Take . . . . .Elaine Paige

Why Don't We Run Away . . . . .Nancy LaMott

With Every Breath I Take . . . . .Nancy LaMott

Just in Time for Christmas . . . . .Nancy LaMott

Stay with Me (Christmas) . . . . .Nancy LaMott

It's Better with a Band . . . . .Barbara Cook

The Ingenue . . . . .Barbara Cook

Inbetween Goodbyes . . . . .Barbara Cook

Another Mister Right . . . . .Barbara Cook

You Can Always Count on Me . . . . .Randy Graff

With Every Breath I Take . . . . .Helen Reddy

Reflection . . . . .Vanessa Mae

Mr. Sunshine . . . . .Pamala Stanley

What I Like Is You . . . . .Pamala Stanley

Only You Can Reach Me . . . . .Pamala Stanley

I Feel a Rush . . . . .Margo Thomas

Move It . . . . .Margo Thomas

Stop Me . . . . .Margo Thomas

Movie Queen . . . . .Kathy Baker

ABOUT THE SONGS
by David Zippel

"It's Better with a Band" – Wally Harper and I wrote this song for Barbara Cook's 1980 Carnegie Hall concert. It was intended to open the show and to introduce the members of the onstage orchestra one by one. For some reason it ended up as the finale.

"Why Don't We Run Away" (music by Bryon Sommers) was one of the first songs I wrote lyrics for when I moved to New York. Nancy LaMott was the first to record it many years later on her first CD.

"Another Mr. Right" is from *Going Hollywood*, an as yet unproduced musical adaptation of Moss Hart and George S. Kaufman's *Once in a Lifetime*. Nancy LaMott did the demo; Christine Ebersole did the workshop.

"With Every Breath I Take" (from *City of Angels*) was the second song Cy Coleman and I wrote for the show. It was to be sung by a nightclub singer in a flashback. She was the great love of the private detective, the story's central character, and the words she sings are intended to reflect his feelings for her. The instant Cy played me the melody he had just completed I thought it was exceptionally beautiful. I very much wanted the lyric I wrote for it to please Cy and I was very aware that I was in the "on approval" stage of our collaboration. I came up with the title on the spot about which Cy was enthusiastic. During the two weeks leading up to our next scheduled meeting I wrote 12 different lyrics. When we next met I put the pile of lyrics on his piano with the first one I had written (which was the one I liked best) on top. Cy played and sang it through without pausing, and said, "This is wonderful." I surreptitiously removed the other 11 lyrics as Cy called Larry Gelbart in California to sing our new song for him over the phone. And we never looked back.

"You're Nothing Without Me" (music by Cy Coleman, from *City of Angels*) – I have a special fondness for this song as it is not only the first act finale but the synthesis of Larry, Cy and my work on the show. In it, the fictional detective Stone confronts his creator, the writer Stine. The world of reality and fiction meet for the first time in the show.

"**You Can Always Count on Me**" (music by Cy Coleman, from *City of Angels*) is a duet for two characters played by the same actress. *City of Angels* is a *film noire* movie within a musical, and in the show this song is started by a fictional character in the movie (in black and white) and finished by the real woman (in living color) who inspired the writer to create her fictional alter ego. All without missing a beat. As complicated as this sounds, it was clear as a bell in Michael Blakemore's elegant production with ingeniously designed sets by Robin Wagner, costumes by Florence Klotz and lighting by Paul Gallo. And *both* ladies were unforgettably brought to life by Randy Graff.

"**How Can I Win?**" (music by Marvin Hamlisch, from *The Goodbye Girl*) – This song was written for the lowest moment of Paula, the show's central character. The challenge was to make it a song of self-discovery rather than self-pity.

"**Just in Time for Christmas**" – One of Nancy LaMott's dreams had always been to do a Christmas album. David Friedman and I wrote this song for Nancy which became the title of that, her fourth CD.

"**Go the Distance**" (from Walt Disney's *Hercules*) was a very late addition to the film. Due to some changes, we found ourselves needing to replace the song that introduced young Hercules. We also found ourselves without a single. Alan Menken thought we should try to solve both of these problems and also create the musical theme for the score. Happily, we did.

"**Reflection**" (from Walt Disney's *Mulan*) was sung by Lea Salonga within the animated film. A pop version during the end credits was performed by a then unknown 16-year-old: Christina Aguilera.

"**Born for You**" (music by David Pomeranz) was written for but not used in a film adaptation of *Romeo and Juliet*. As a result of David Pomeranz's recording of the song, it became the most performed song in the Philippines in 2000. Go figure.

"**It Started with a Dream**" is from *Pamela's First Musical*, which Cy Coleman and I are writing with Wendy Wasserstein based upon her popular children's book.

ANOTHER MR. RIGHT

Music by JONATHAN SHEFFER
Lyrics by DAVID ZIPPEL

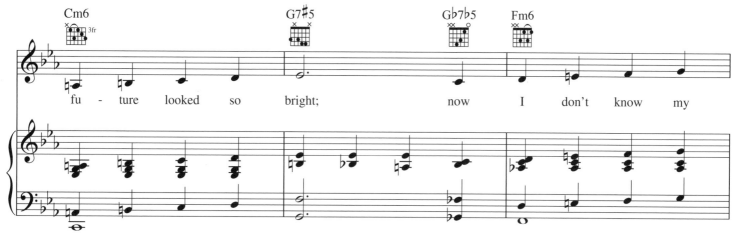

fu - ture looked so bright; now I don't know my

left from my right. An -

oth - er Mis - ter Right left, we're call - ing it a day. _ An - oth - er Mis - ter Right left, the

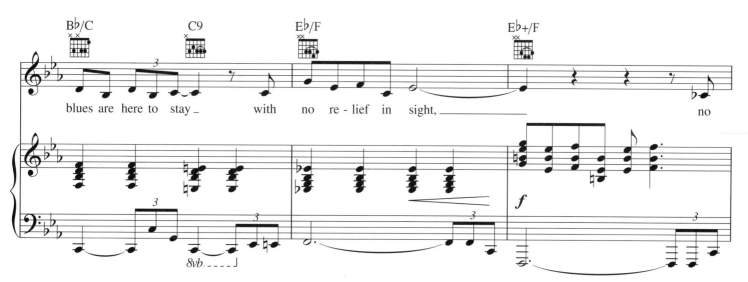

blues are here to stay _ with no re - lief in sight, _____ no

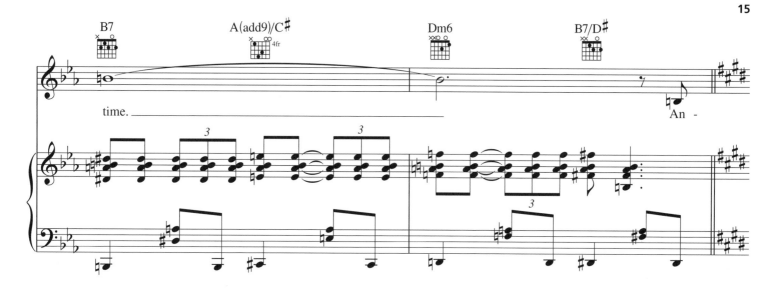

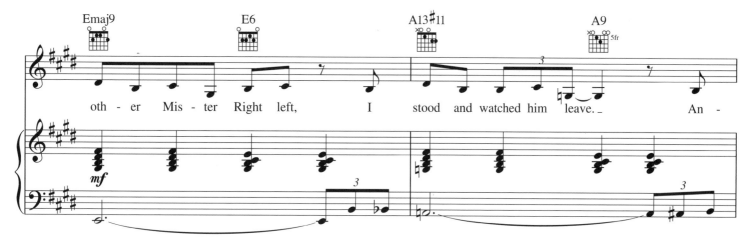

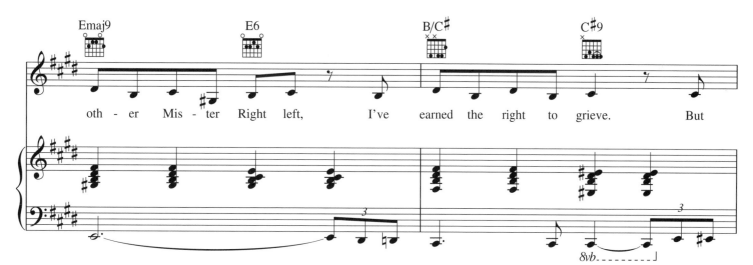

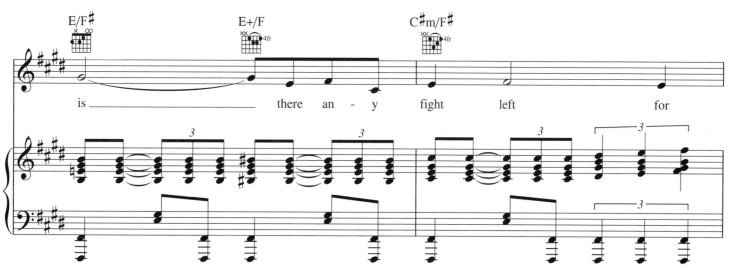

BORN FOR YOU

Music by DAVID POMERANZ
Lyrics by DAVID ZIPPEL

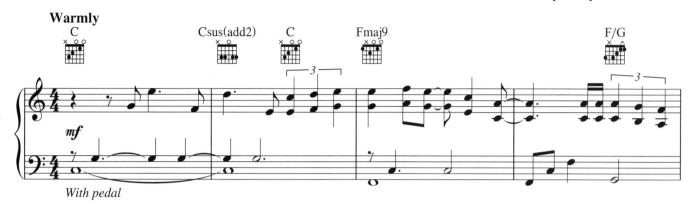

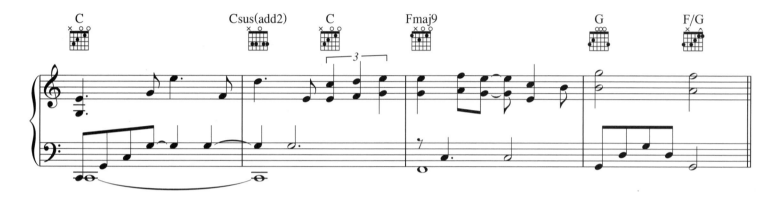

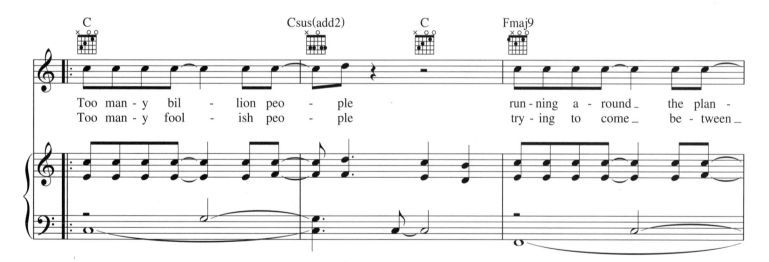

Too man-y bil - lion peo - ple   run-ning a-round_ the plan-
Too man-y fool-ish peo - ple   try-ing to come_ be-tween_

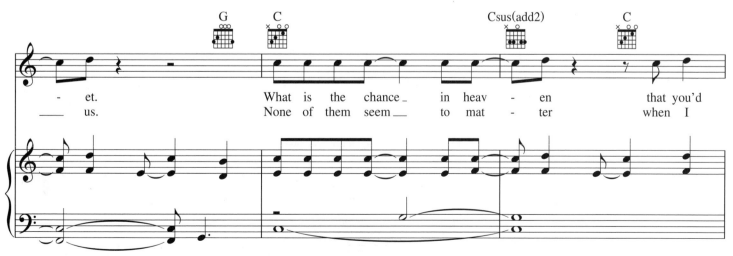

-et.   What is the chance_ in heav - en   that you'd
__ us.   None of them seem__ to mat - ter   when I

find your way __ to me? __   Tell me, what is this sweet __ sen - sa -
look in - to __ your eyes. __   Now I know __ why I __ be - long __

- tion?   It's a mir - a - cle __ that's hap - pened.   Though I
__ here;   in your arms I found __ the an - swer.   Some - how

search for an ex - pla - na - tion,   on - ly one thing it __ could be, __
noth - ing would seem __ so wrong __ here   if they'd on - ly re - a - lize __

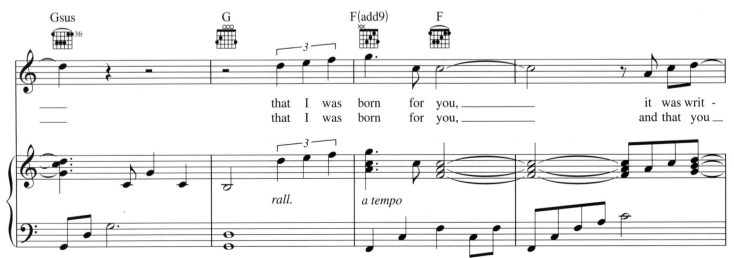

that I was born for you, _____   it was writ -
that I was born for you, _____   and that you __

rall.   a tempo

- ten in the stars. Yes, I was born for you,
— were born for me, and in this ran - dom world

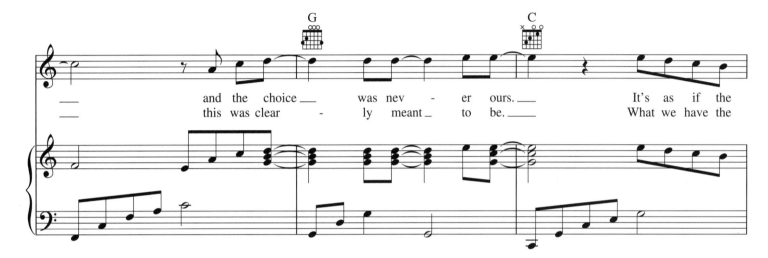

— and the choice was nev - er ours. It's as if the
— this was clear - ly meant to be. What we have the

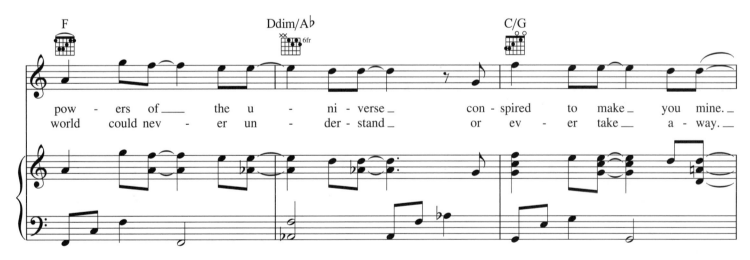

pow - ers of the u - ni - verse con - spired to make you mine.
world could nev - er un - der - stand or ev - er take a - way.

And till the day I die, I bless the day that I

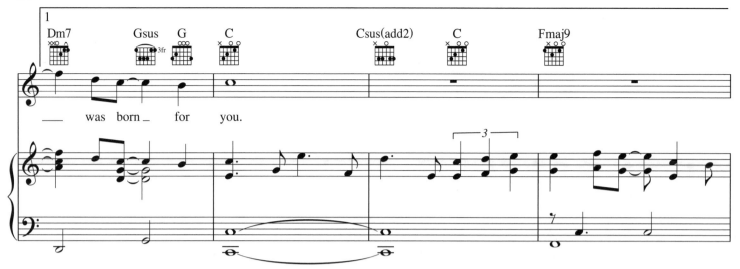

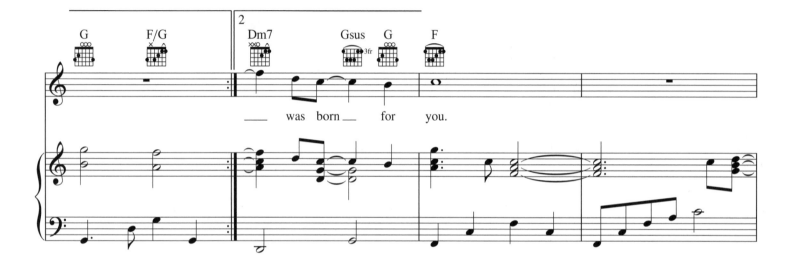

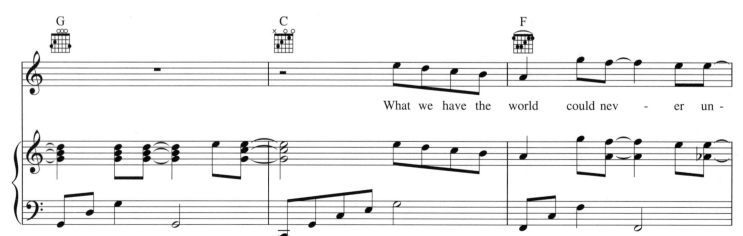

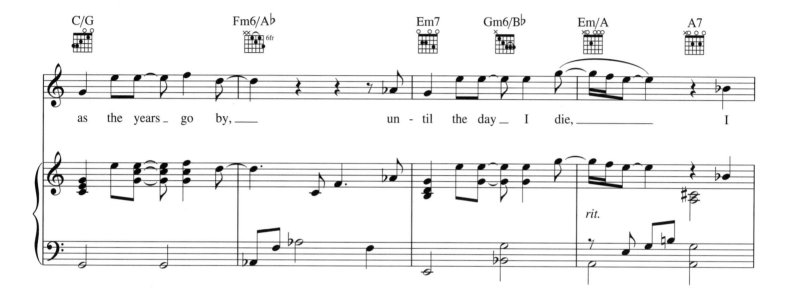

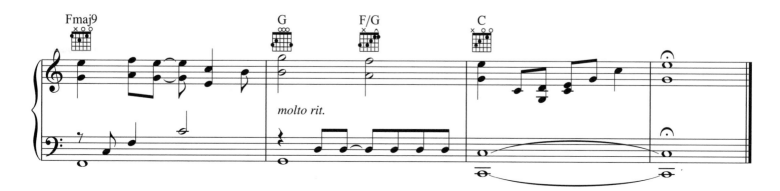

GO THE DISTANCE

(Pop Version)

from Walt Disney Pictures' HERCULES
As Performed by Michael Bolton

Music by ALAN MENKEN
Lyrics by DAVID ZIPPEL

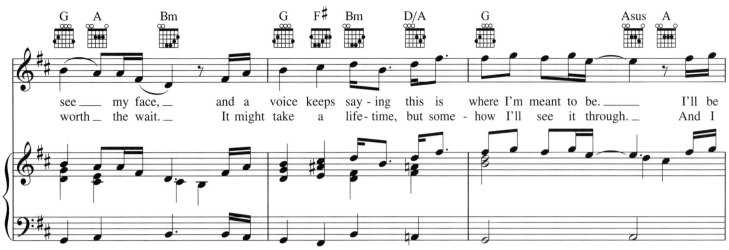

see __ my face, __ and a voice keeps say-ing this is where I'm meant to be. __ I'll be
worth __ the wait. __ It might take a life-time, but some-how I'll see it through. __ And I

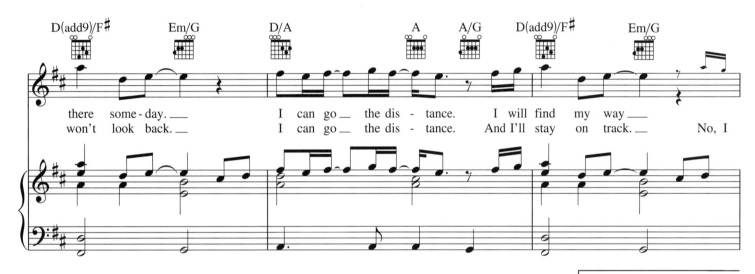

there some-day. __ I can go __ the dis - tance. I will find my way __
won't look back. __ I can go __ the dis - tance. And I'll stay on track. __ No, I

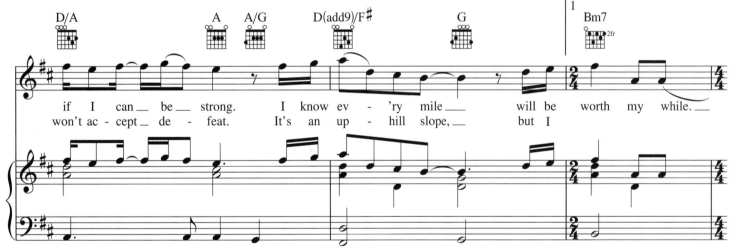

if I can __ be __ strong. I know ev-'ry mile __ will be worth my while. __
won't ac-cept __ de - feat. It's an up-hill slope, __ but I

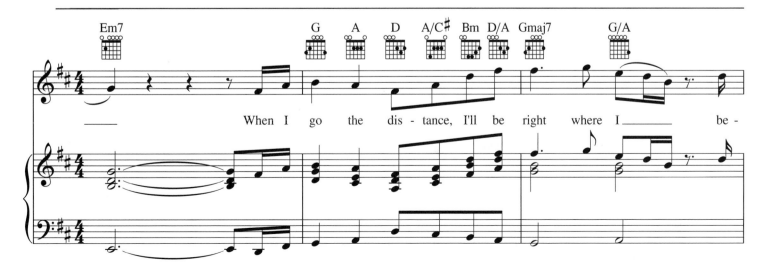

When I go the dis - tance, I'll be right where I __ be -

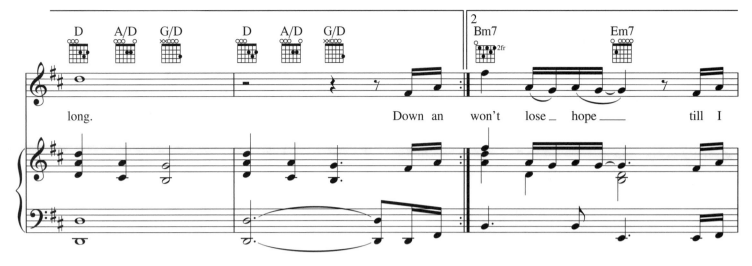

long.
Down an won't lose _ hope ____ till I

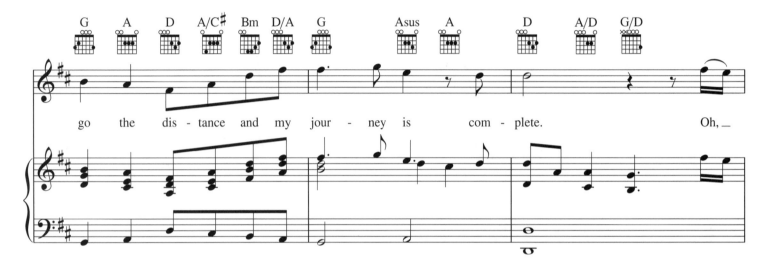

go the dis - tance and my jour - ney is com - plete.
Oh, __

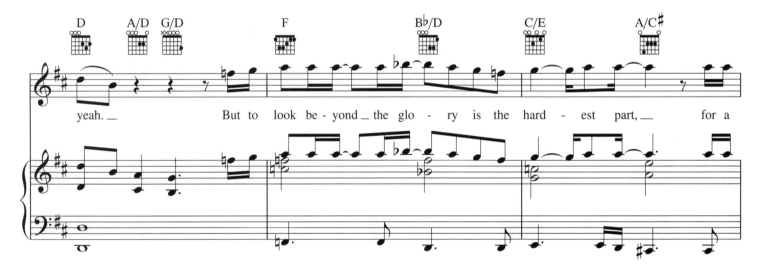

yeah. __
But to look be - yond _ the glo - ry is the hard - est part, __ for a

he - ro's strength __ is meas - ured by his heart.

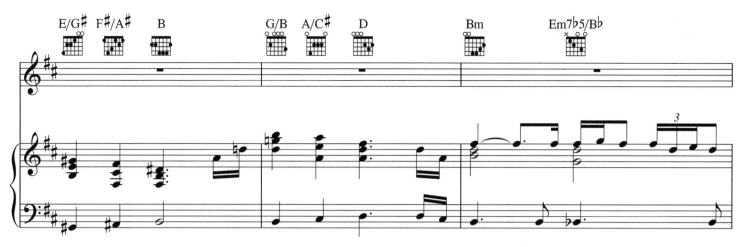

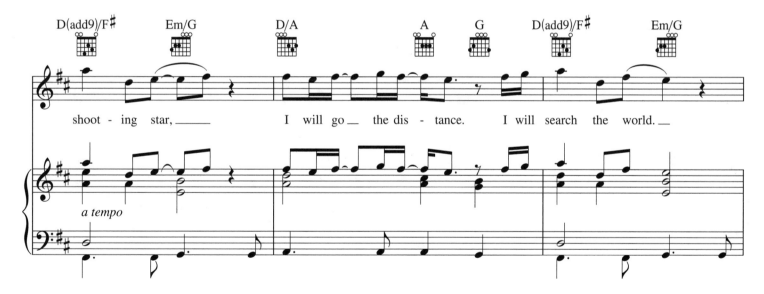

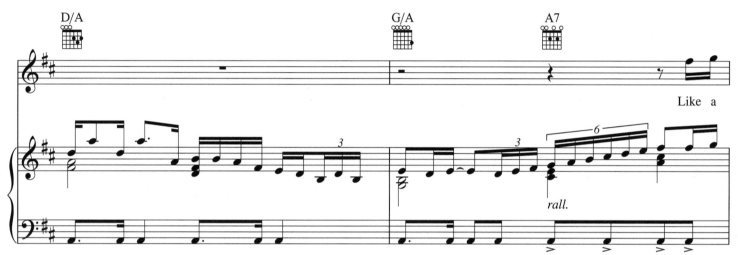

26

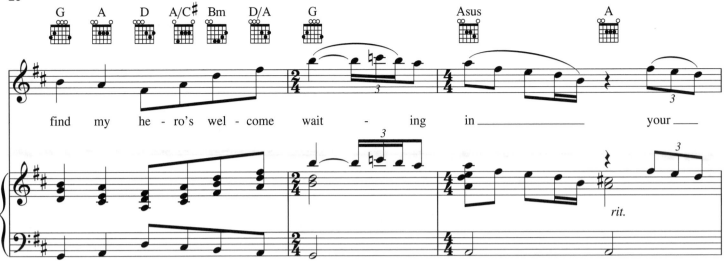

find my he - ro's wel - come wait - ing in _____ your ____

Broadly

arms. I will

search the world. __ I will face its harms _____ till I

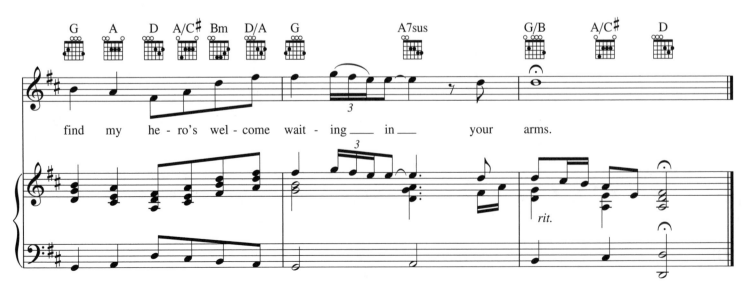

find my he - ro's wel - come wait - ing ___ in ___ your arms.

IT'S BETTER WITH A BAND

Music by WALLY HARPER
Lyrics by DAVID ZIPPEL

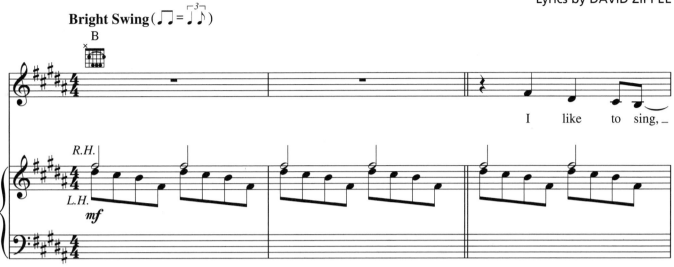

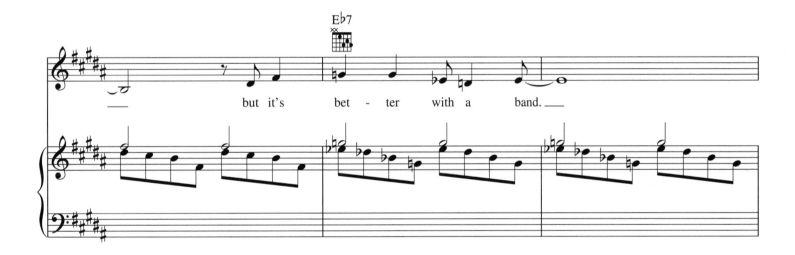

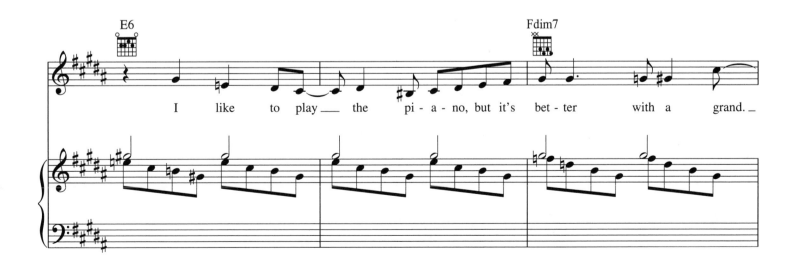

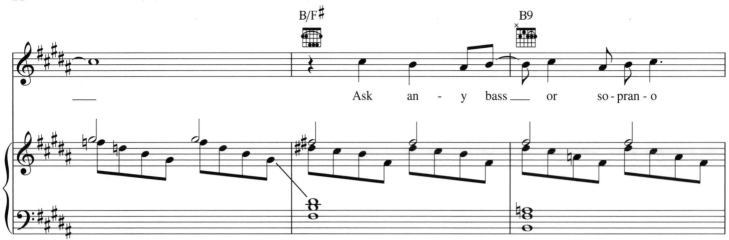

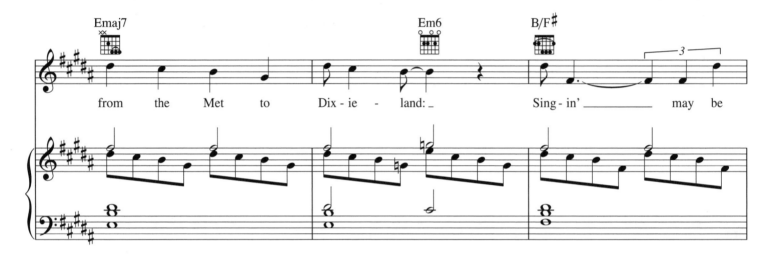

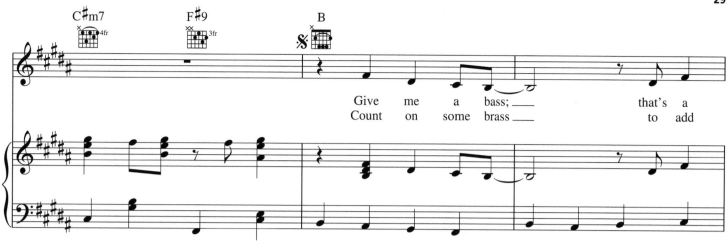

Give me a bass; ___ that's a
Count on some brass ___ to add

per - fect place to start. ___ Then add a drum-
class that does - n't fail. ___ Can't beat the sound _

- mer with rhy - thm and you're sure to reach my heart. ___
___ of a sax that's go - in' up and down the scale. ___

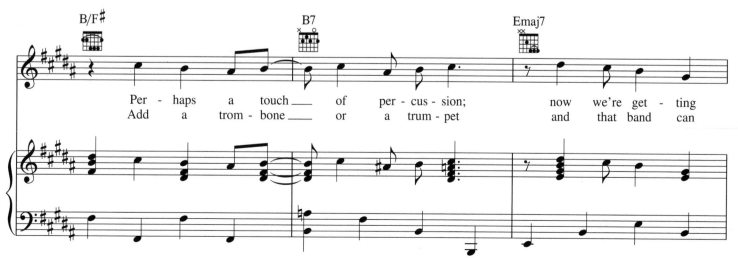

Per - haps a touch ___ of per - cus - sion; now we're get - ting
Add a trom - bone ___ or a trum - pet and that band can

close to art. __ } Sing - in' _____ may be swing - in', _____ but
real - ly wail. __

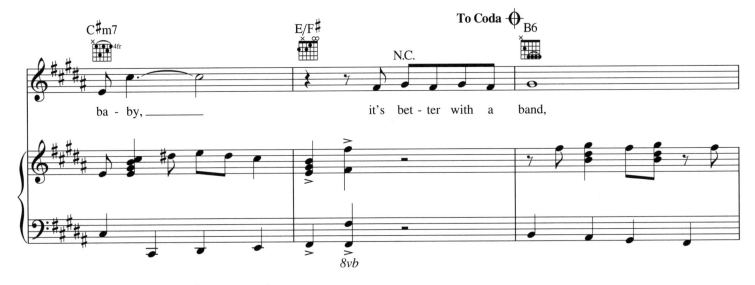

ba - by, _____ it's bet - ter with a band,

To Coda ⊕

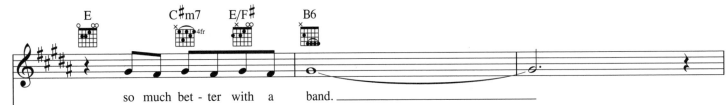

so much bet - ter with a band. _____

Hey, _____ we could use a clar - i - net __ or two __

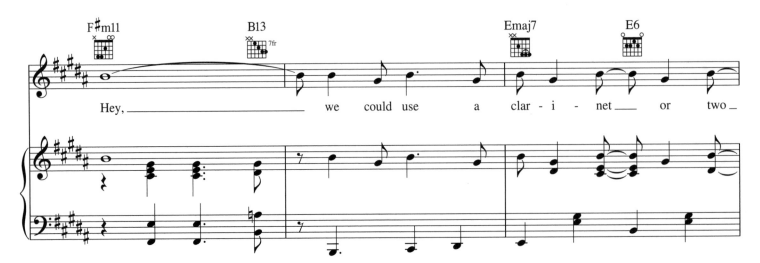

31

to start out. Say, that sounds so good that

e - ven Ben - ny Good - man would eat his heart out.

CODA

band.

Hear those fel - las im - pro - vis - in'.

Can't _____ you feel your spir-its ris - in'? _____

When _____ they real-ly got it go-in' strong, _____

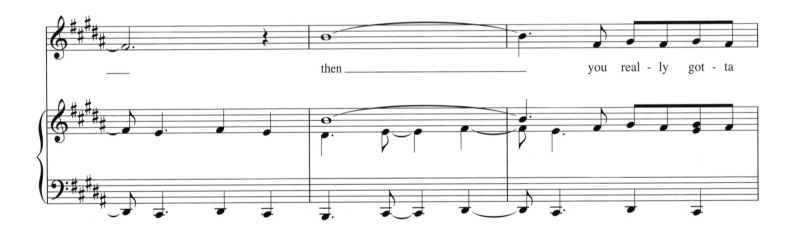

then _____ you real-ly got-ta

sing a - long. _____ Throw in a flute; ___
No band has wings ___

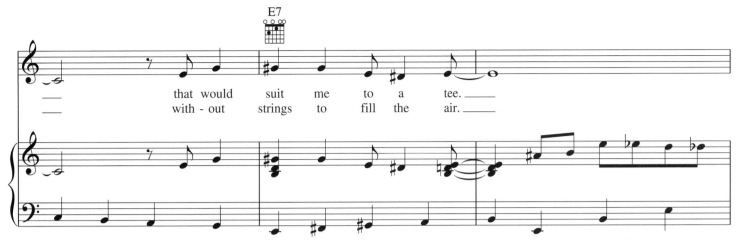

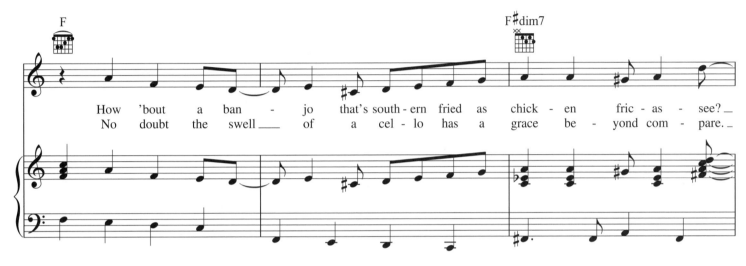

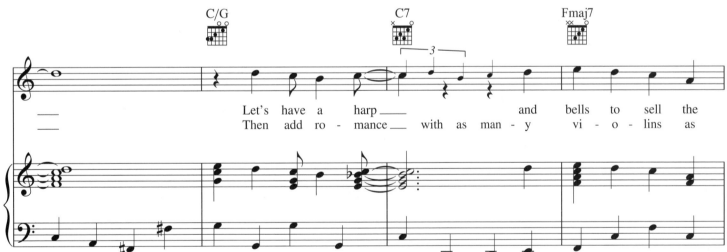

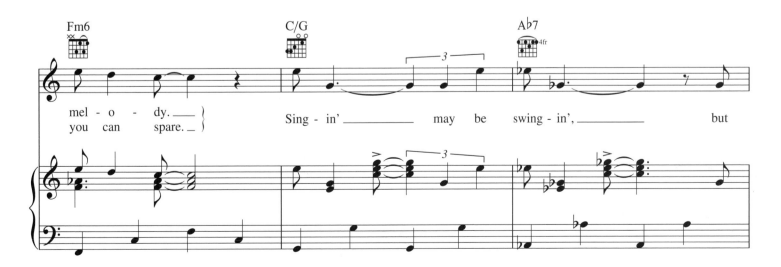

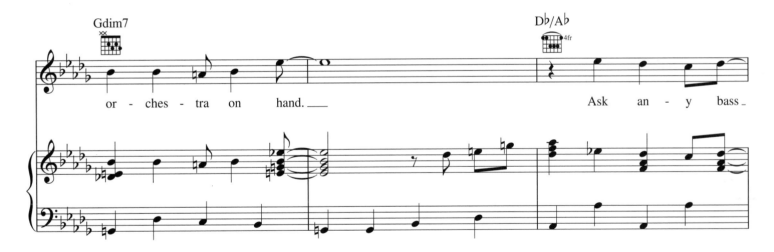

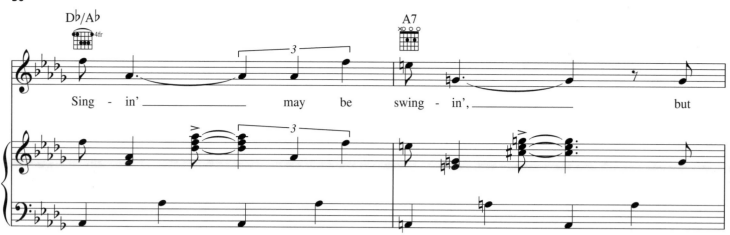

Sing - in' _____ may be swing - in', _____ but

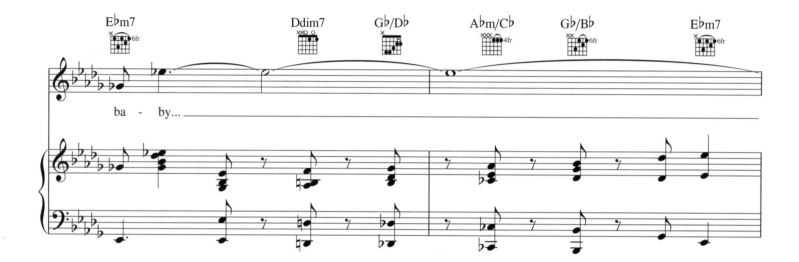

ba - by... _____

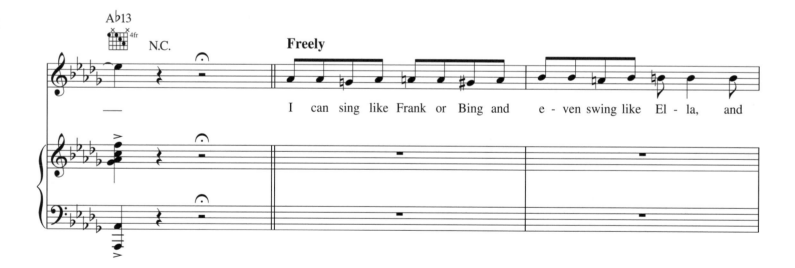

I can sing like Frank or Bing and e - ven swing like El - la, and

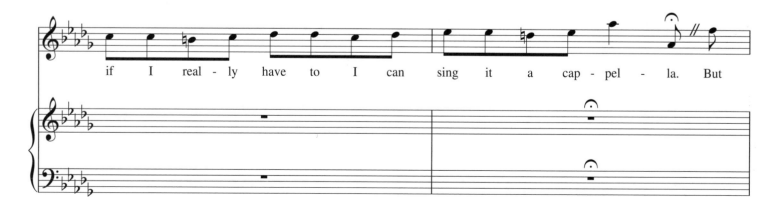

if I real - ly have to I can sing it a cap - pel - la. But

HOW CAN I WIN?
from THE GOODBYE GIRL

Music by MARVIN HAMLISCH
Lyrics by DAVID ZIPPEL

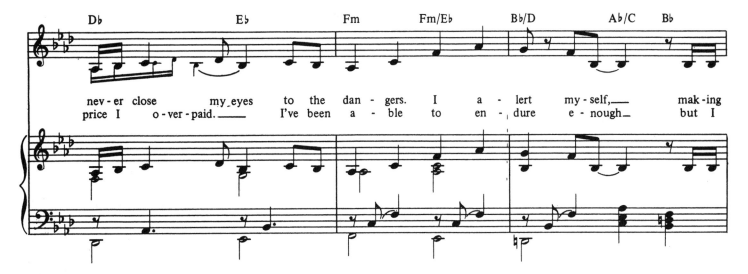

nev - er close my eyes to the dan - gers. I a - lert my - self,___ mak - ing
price I o - ver - paid.___ I've been a - ble to en - dure e - nough___ but I

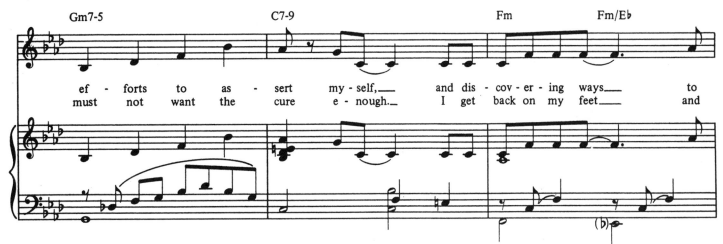

ef - forts to as - sert my - self,___ and dis - cov - er - ing ways___ to
must not want the cure e - nough.___ I get back on my feet___ and

hurt my - self___ that no one else has tried.
sure e - nough,___ my hopes and fears col - lide.

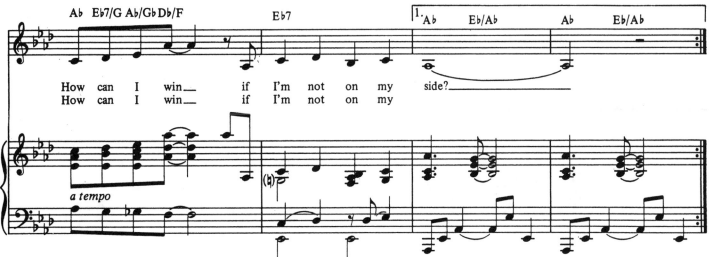

How can I win___ if I'm not on my side?___
How can I win___ if I'm not on my

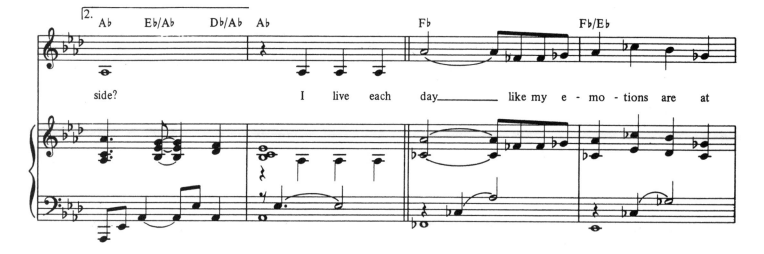

side? I live each day____ like my e - mo - tions are at

war, but I don't re - mem - ber____ an - y - more____ just who or what I'm fight - ing

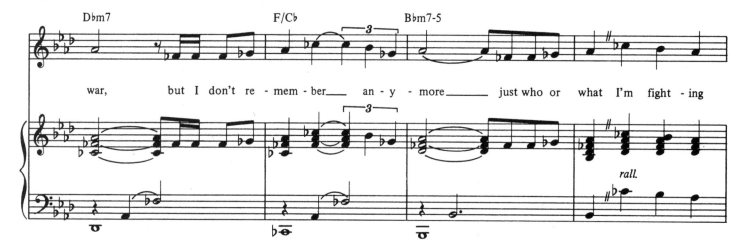

for. ____ When will de - light be mine a - gain?__ Will it

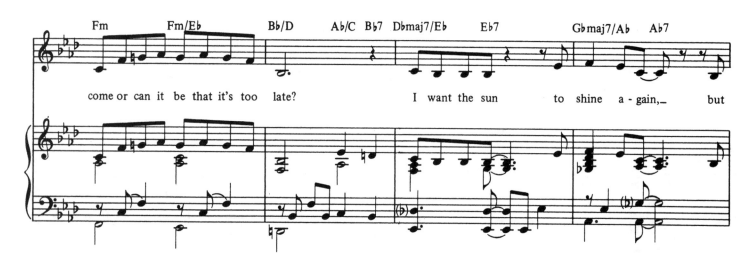

come or can it be that it's too late? I want the sun to shine a - gain,__ but

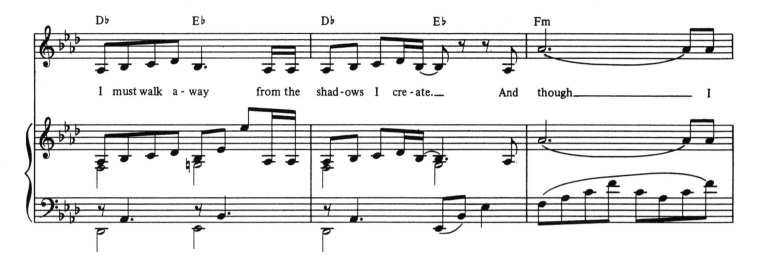

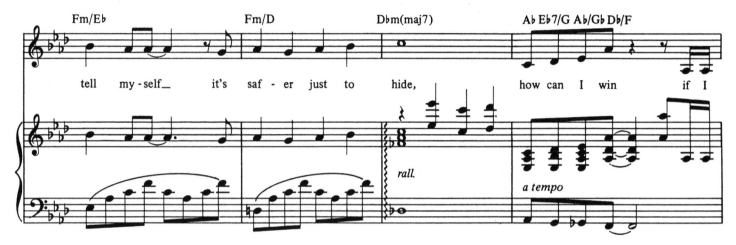

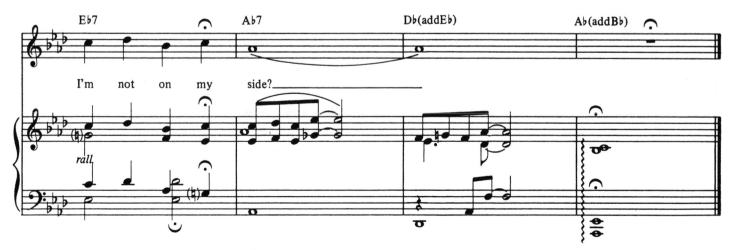

IT STARTED WITH A DREAM

(from PAMELA'S FIRST MUSICAL)

Music by CY COLEMAN
Lyrics by DAVID ZIPPEL

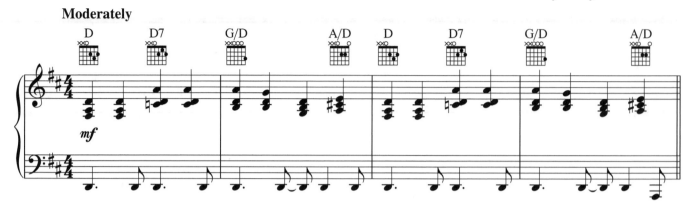

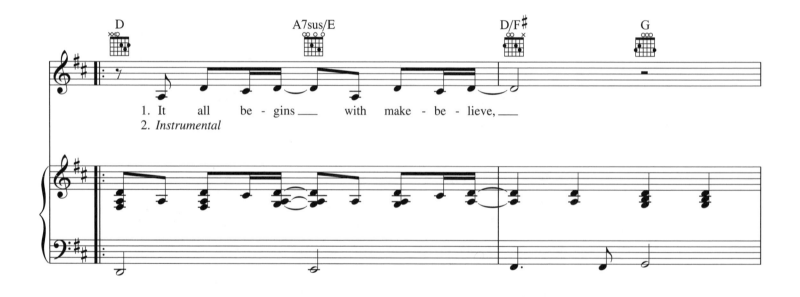

1. It all be-gins ___ with make-be-lieve, ___
2. Instrumental

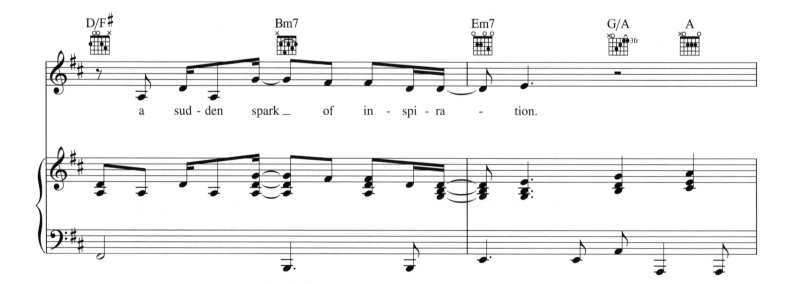

a sud-den spark ___ of in-spi-ra - tion.

And ev-'ry note of ev-'ry theme ___ start-ed with a dream ___

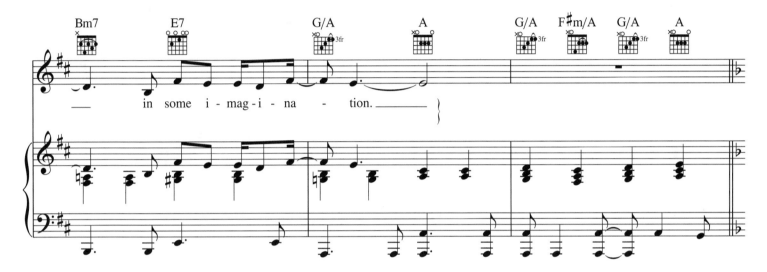

___ in some i-mag-i-na - tion. ___

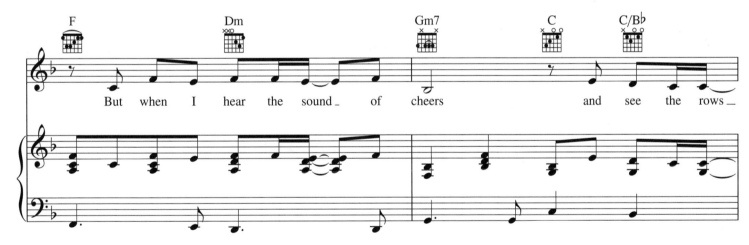

But when I hear the sound ___ of cheers and see the rows ___

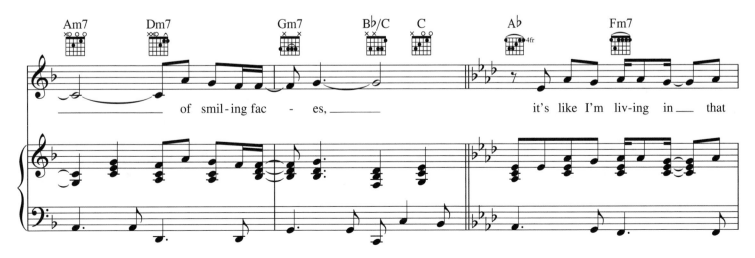

___ of smil-ing fac - es, ___ it's like I'm liv-ing in ___ that

44

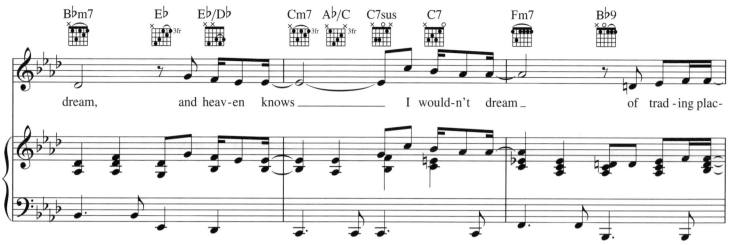

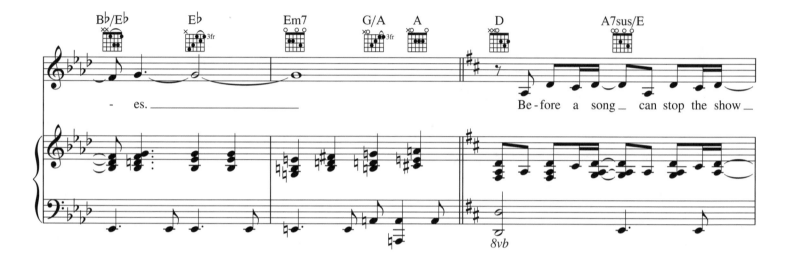

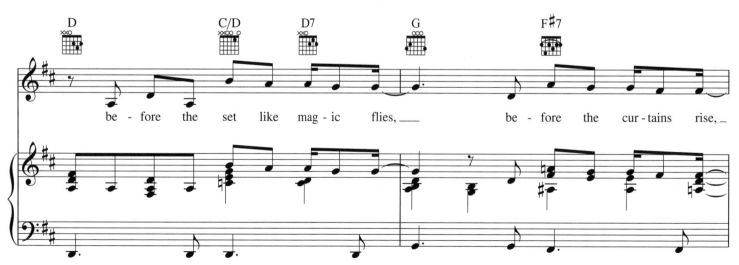

JUST IN TIME FOR CHRISTMAS

Music by DAVID FRIEDMAN
Lyrics by DAVID ZIPPEL

Pop Ballad

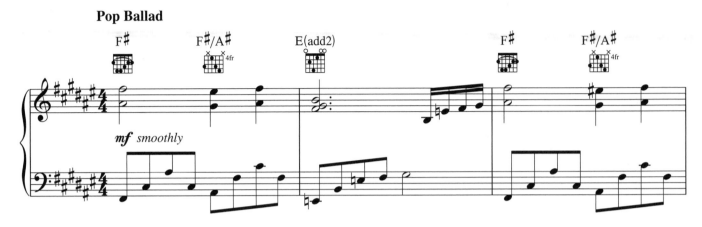

They had decked the malls _ and trimmed the town _ with

plas-tic trees 'til the world was just a gi-ant re-tail maze. 'Tis the

sea - son ____ when you turn your thoughts to peo - ple you can't please, when you

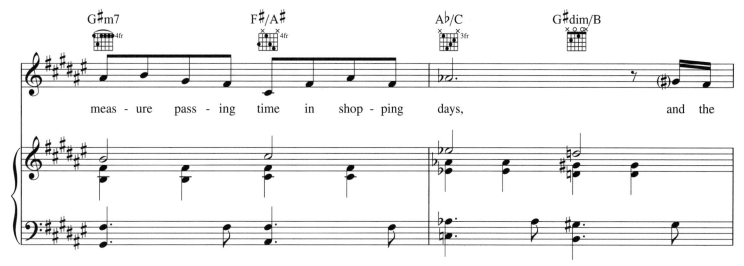

meas - ure pass - ing time in shop - ping days, and the

hol - i - days ____ were some - thing ____ to get through. But the

thing I had - n't count - ed on ____ was you.

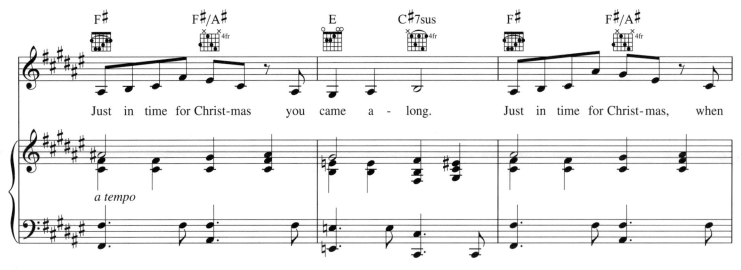

Just in time for Christ-mas you came a-long. Just in time for Christ-mas, when

ev-'ry-thing felt wrong and I was sure my faith had all run out.

Just in time for Christ-mas you showed me what Christ-mas is a-bout.

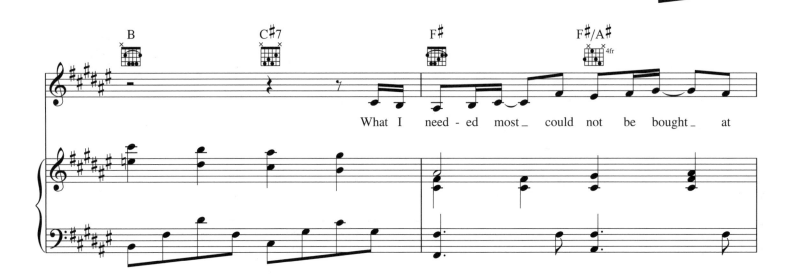

What I need-ed most_ could not be bought_ at

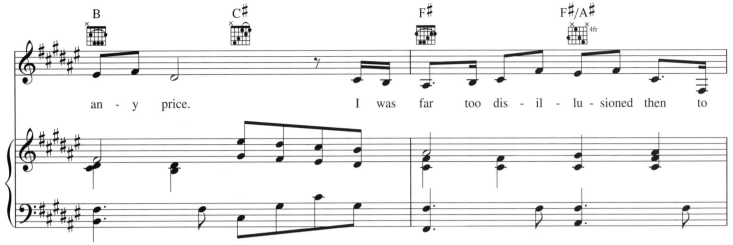

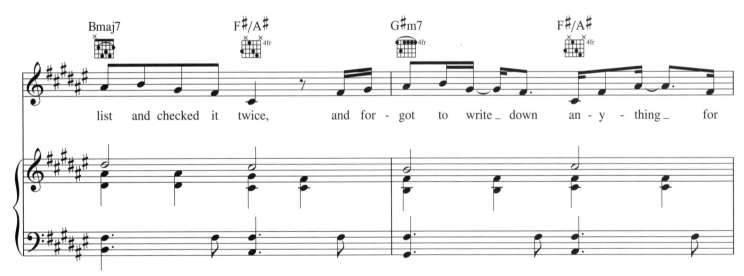

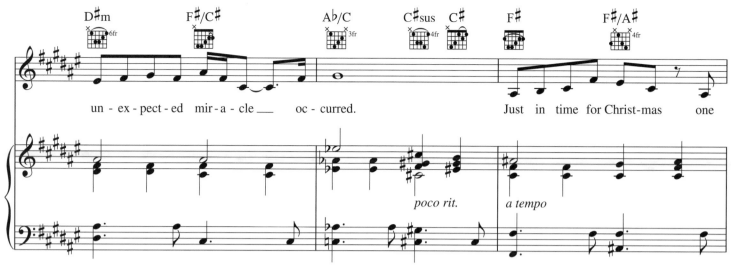

un - ex - pect - ed mir - a - cle ___ oc - curred.
Just in time for Christ-mas one

poco rit.   *a tempo*

si - lent night,   just in time for Christ-mas
you filled my life with light,   and

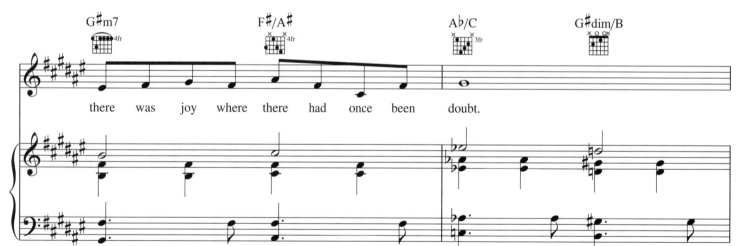

there was joy where there had once been doubt.

Just in time for Christ - mas   you showed me what Christ - mas is a -

bout. _____ And all at once the

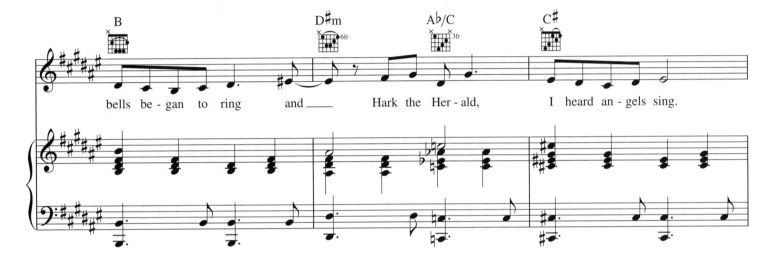

bells be - gan to ring and ____ Hark the Her - ald, I heard an - gels sing.

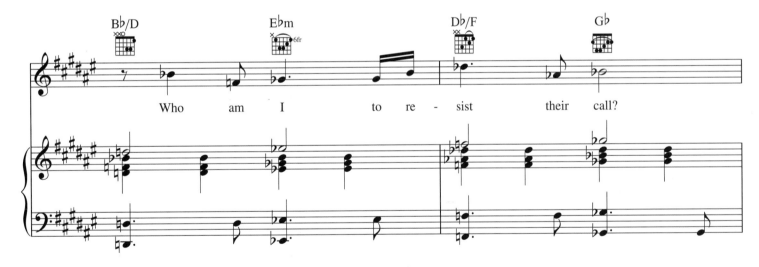

Who am I to re - sist their call?

You brought me the great - est gift of all. _____

52

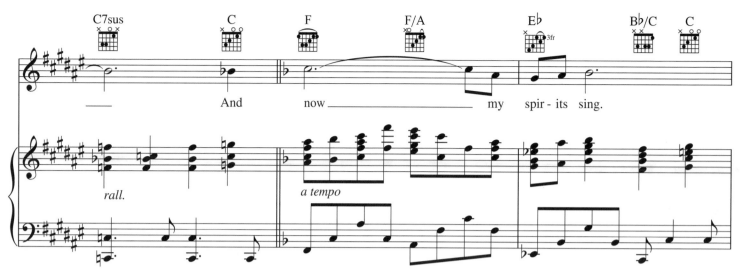

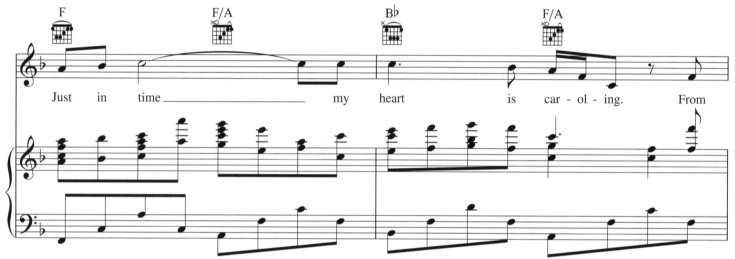

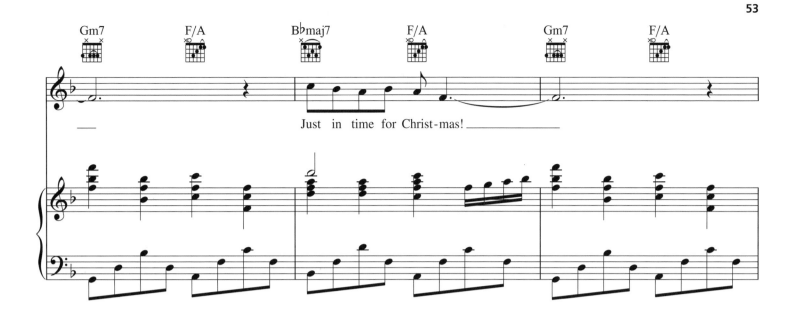

Just in time for Christ-mas! _____

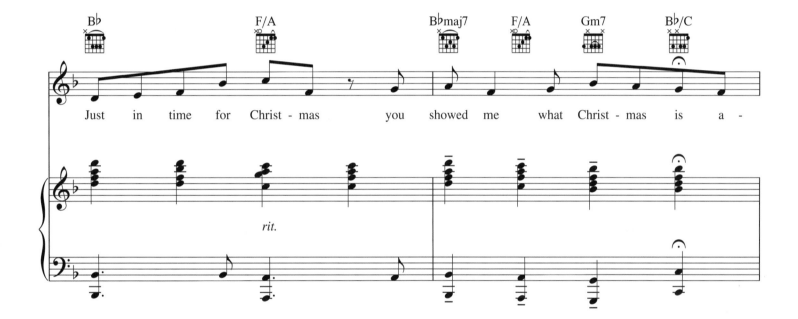

Just in time for Christ - mas you showed me what Christ - mas is a -

rit.

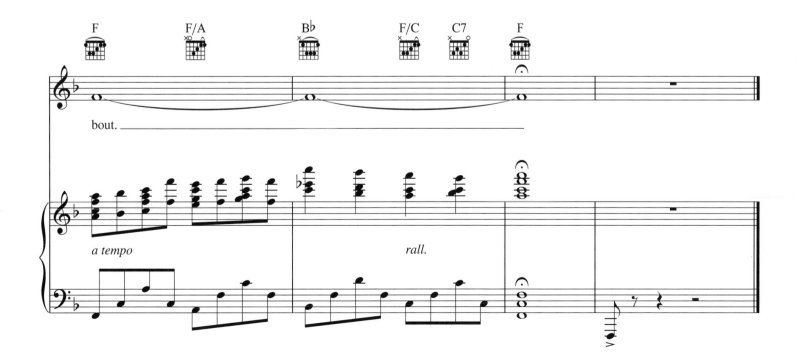

bout. _____

a tempo   *rall.*

REFLECTION
(Pop Version)
from Walt Disney Pictures' MULAN
As Performed by Christina Aguilera

Music by MATTHEW WILDER
Lyrics by DAVID ZIPPEL

Look at me, you may think you see who I

real-ly am, but you'll nev-er know me. Ev-'ry day it's

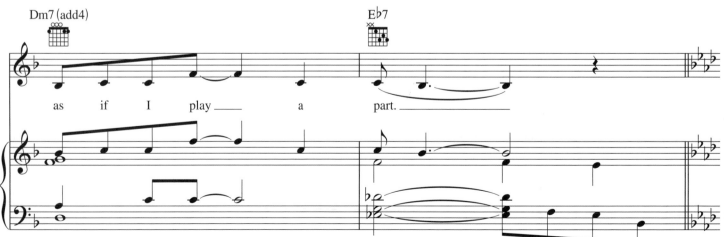

as if I play a part.

Now I see ___ if I wear a mask ___ I can
But some - how ___ I will show the world ___ what's in -

fool ___ the world, ___ but I can - not fool my ___ heart.
side ___ my heart ___ and be loved for who I ___ am.

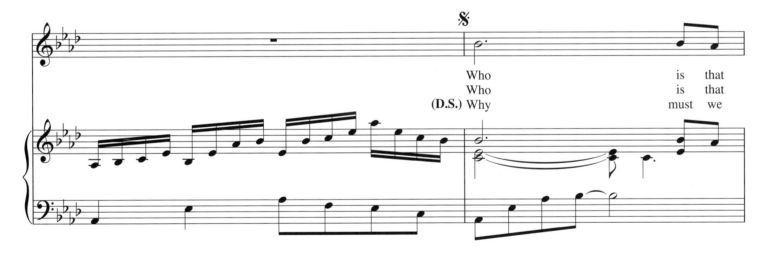

Who ___ is that
Who ___ is that
(D.S.) Why ___ must we

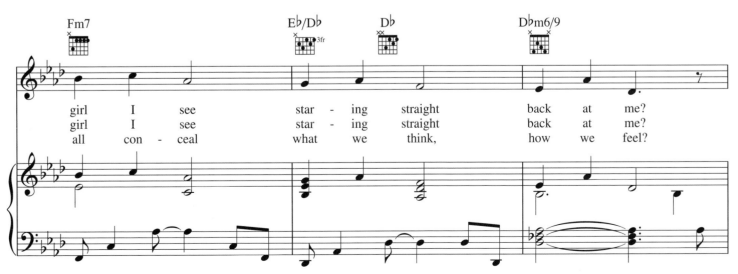

girl I see star - ing straight back at me?
girl I see star - ing straight back at me?
all con - ceal what we think, how we feel?

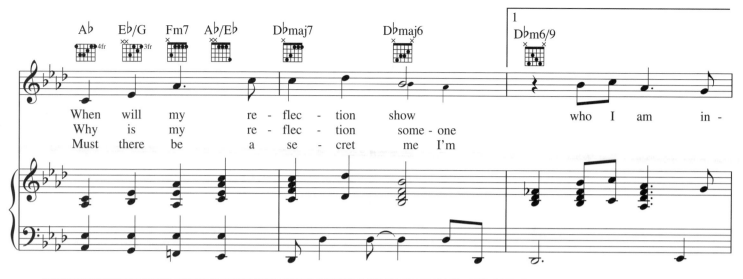

When will my re - flec - tion show
Why is my re - flec - tion show some - one
Must there be a se - cret me I'm

who I am in -

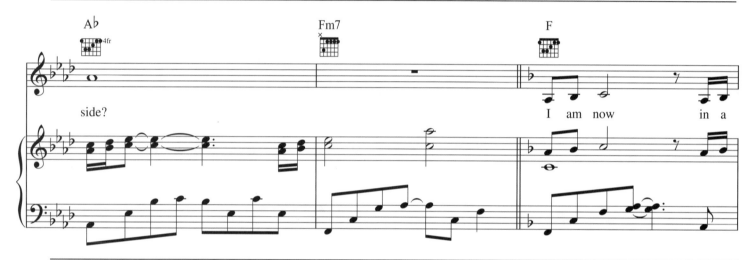

side?

I am now in a

world where I___ have to hide my heart ___ and what I be - lieve in.

I
forced
don't to
know?
hide?

Must I pre - tend that I'm some - one else
I won't pre - tend that I'm some - one else

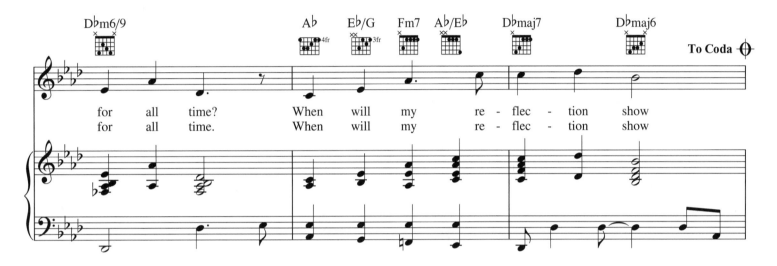

for all time? When will my re - flec - tion show
for all time. When will my re - flec - tion show

To Coda ⊕

who I am?___ In - side,___ there's a heart that must be

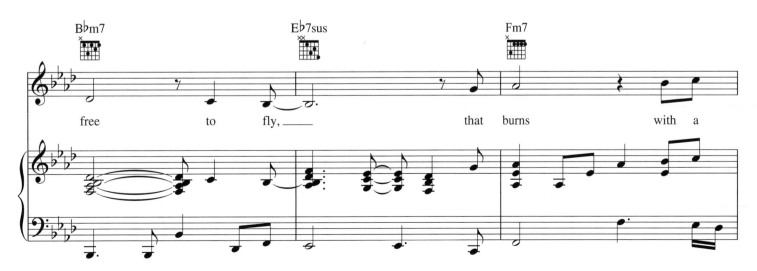

free to fly, _____ that burns with a

D.S. al Coda
(take 2nd ending)

need to know the rea - son _____ why. _____

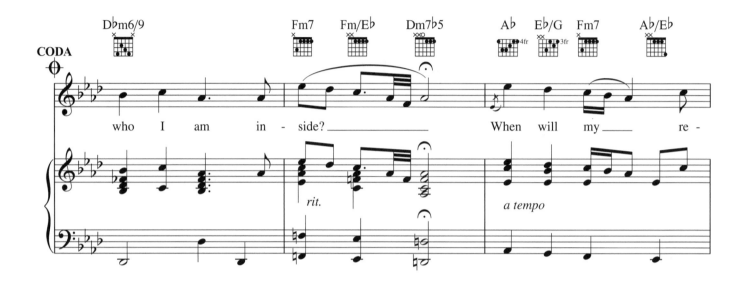

who I am in - side? _____ When will my _____ re-

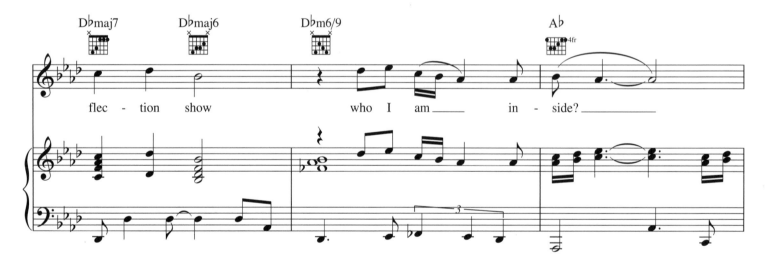

flec - tion show who I am _____ in - side? _____

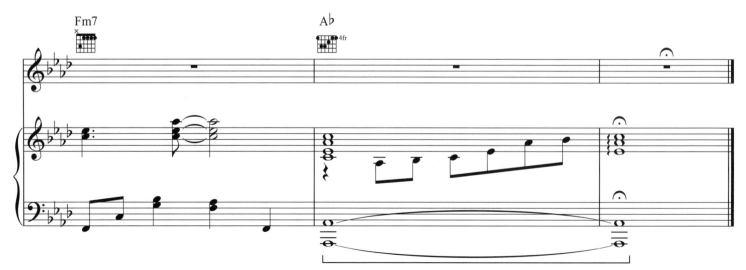

YOU CAN ALWAYS COUNT ON ME

Music by CY COLEMAN
Lyrics by DAVID ZIPPEL

right,   but what good does it do me a - lone on a Sat - ur - day night?

Moderately

I   don't need a map, I nat -'ral - ly head for the dead end street._
mat - ter of fact, if you want   an   ill - fat - ed love af - fair,_
my kind of dame no doubt will   die   out like the   di - no - saurs,_

You   can al - ways count   on   me._   I'm
you   can al - ways count   on   me._   Though
you   can al - ways count   on   me._   I'm

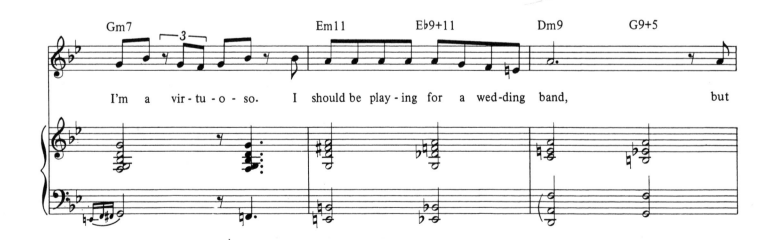

they're no wed-ding rings at-tached,_ though you can bet they're strings at-tached._

Though

Guess who they ex-pect to see?_

You can al-ways count on, bet a large a-mount on, you can al-ways count on me!_

cresc. to end

WHY DON'T WE RUN AWAY

Music by BRYON SOMMERS
Lyrics by DAVID ZIPPEL

Why don't we run ___ a - way ___ where ___ no one can find ___ us? We'll nev - er

look be - hind us. Why don't we run ___ a - way? ___ You see, ___ my

love for you has run a - way _____ with

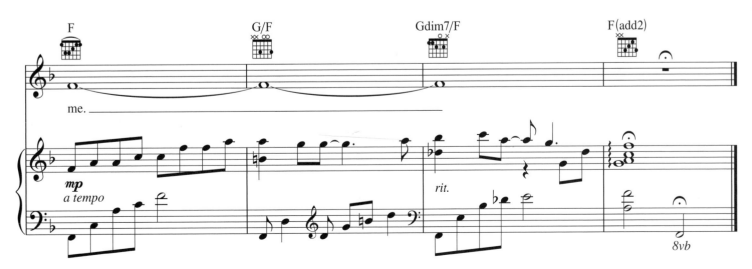

me. _____

WITH EVERY BREATH I TAKE

Music by CY COLEMAN
Lyrics by DAVID ZIPPEL

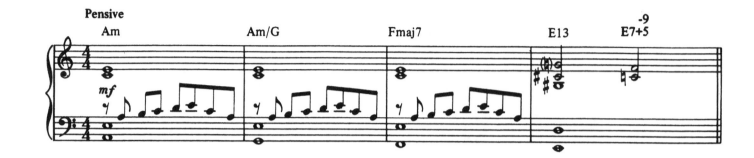

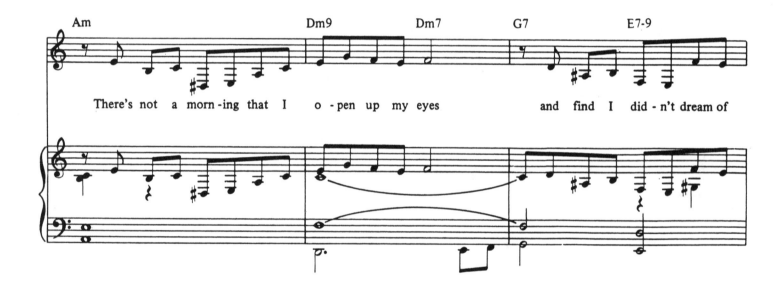

There's not a morn-ing that I o-pen up my eyes and find I did-n't dream of

you. With-out a warn-ing, though it's nev-er a sur-prise, soon as I a-wake

thoughts of you a - rise with ev - 'ry breath I take._____

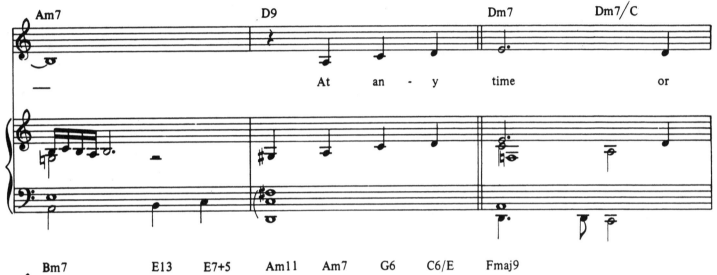

At an - y time or

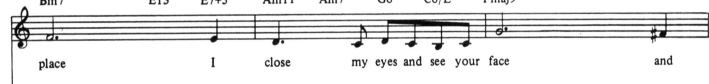

place I close my eyes and see your face and

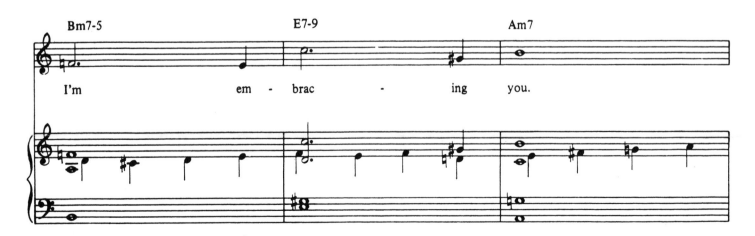

I'm em - brac - ing you.

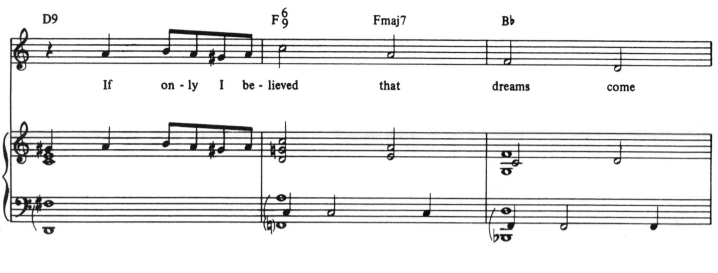

If on-ly I be-lieved that dreams come

true. Dar - ling, you were the one who said for-

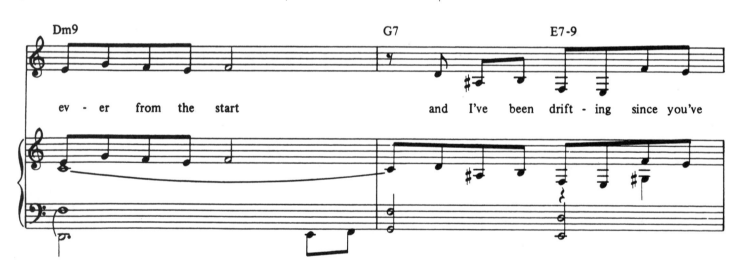

ev - er from the start and I've been drift - ing since you've

gone, out on a lone-ly sea that on-ly you can chart.

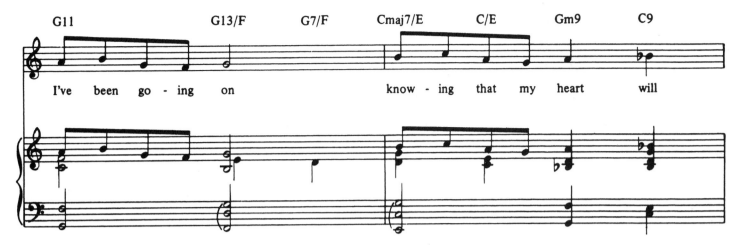

I've been go - ing on

know - ing that my heart will

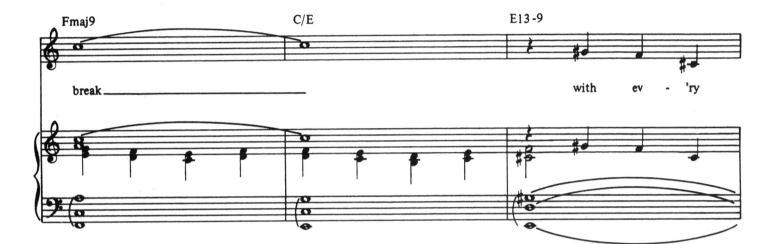

break _____

with ev - 'ry

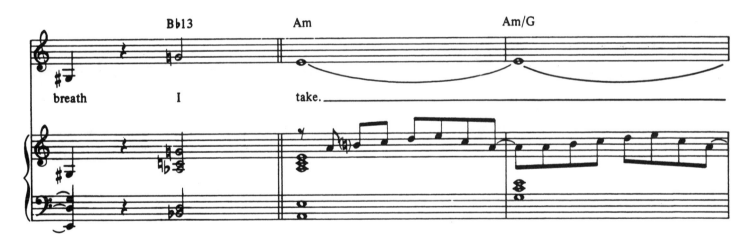

breath   I   take. _____

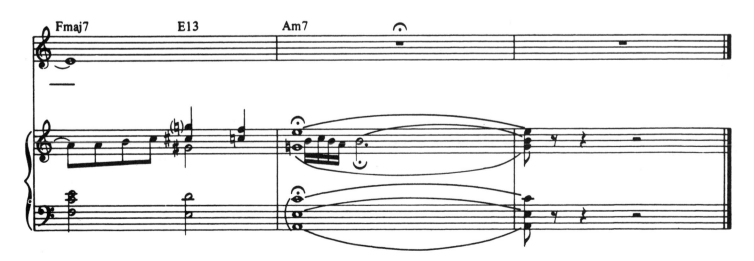

YOU'RE NOTHING WITHOUT ME

Music by CY COLEMAN
Lyrics by DAVID ZIPPEL

Moderately bright

You are some gum - shoe, you just don't think_ well.
You are so jeal - ous of my track rec - ord.

Get this dumb gum - shoe, you come_ from my ink - well.
Tol - stoy, do tell_ us, your fee - ble hack rec - ord.

Is your mouth lone-ly with one foot in __ there?
Your weak knees brand __ you soft and un-sta-ble.

Stone, your brain on-ly holds thoughts __ I put in __ there.
One small threat and __ you fold like __ a card ta-ble.

L'istesso

Just what you are I'll spell out. __
You drool at my ad-ven-tures, __

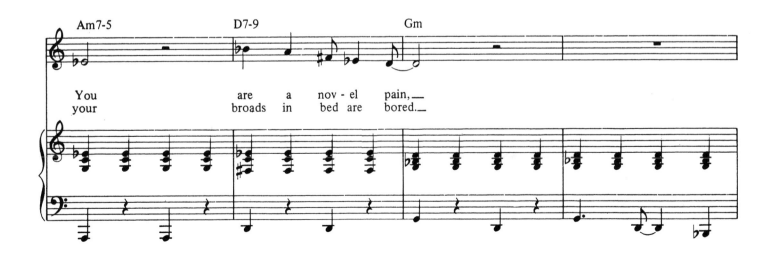

You are a nov-el pain, __
your broads in bed are bored. __

tell you you're out of my mind. A show off, a

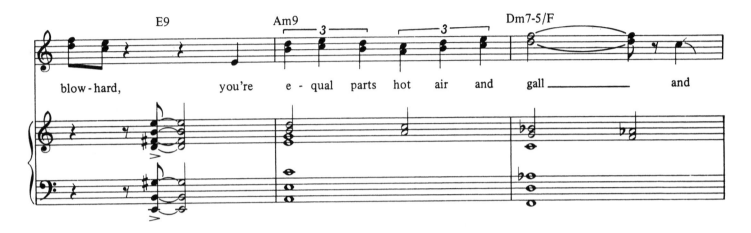

blow-hard, you're e-qual parts hot air and gall _____ and

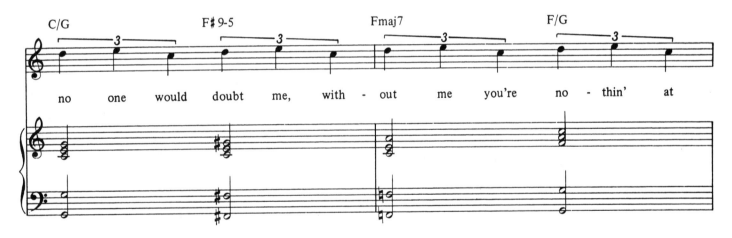

no one would doubt me, with-out me you're no-thin' at

all. _____

76

*Alternate lyrics for "YOU'RE NOTHING WITHOUT ME" (If alternate lyrics are used, begin song at this point.)
**Alternate lyrics for "I'M NOTHING WITHOUT YOU"

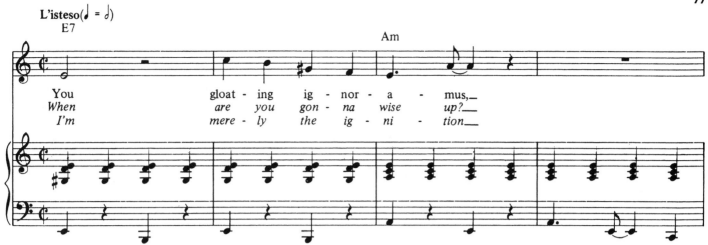

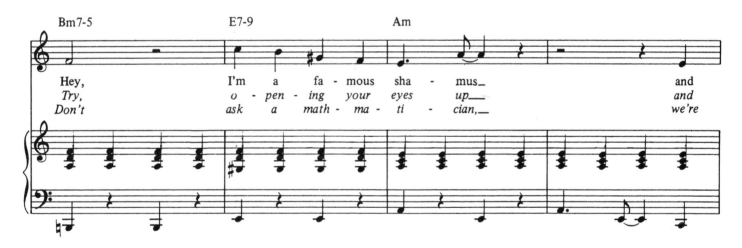

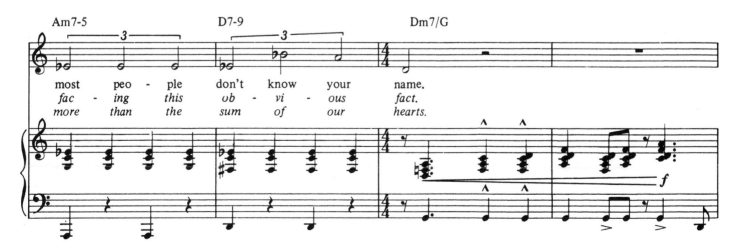

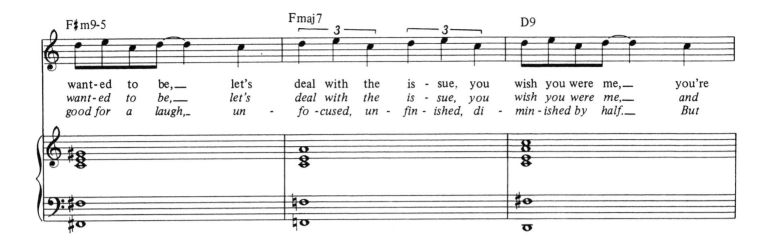

F#m9-5 / Fmaj7 / D9

want-ed to be,__ let's deal with the is - sue, you wish you were me,__ you're
want-ed to be,__ let's deal with the is - sue, you wish you were me,__ and
good for a laugh,__ un - fo -cused, un - fin - ished, di - min -ished by half.__ But

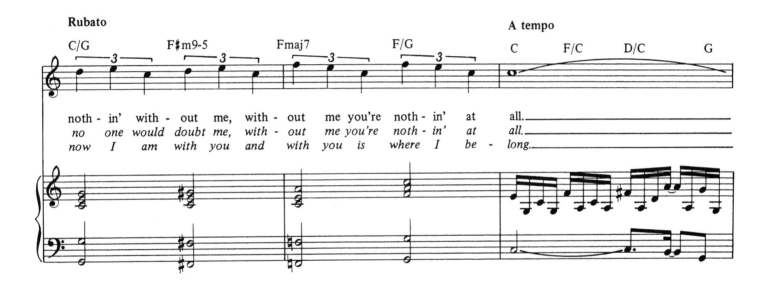

Rubato / **A tempo**

C/G / F#m9-5 / Fmaj7 / F/G / C F/C D/C G

noth - in' with - out me, with - out me you're noth - in' at all._____
no one would doubt me, with - out me you're noth - in' at all._____
now I am with you and with you is where I be - long._____

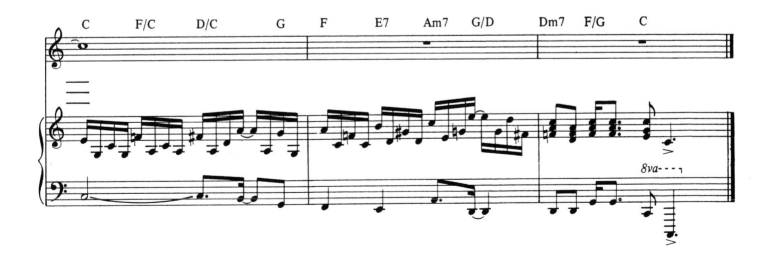

C F/C D/C G F E7 Am7 G/D Dm7 F/G C

8va----